What Makes Me A
JEW?

Adam Woog

**KIDHAVEN
PRESS**™

San Diego • Detroit • New York • San Francisco • Cleveland
New Haven, Conn. • Waterville, Maine • London • Munich

*In memory of my grandparents—
and also for my daughter, Leah, who
(when she was little) once told me that she
liked being "half Jewish and half plain."*

LIBRARY OF CONGRESS CATALOGING-IN-PUBLICATION DATA

Woog, Adam, 1953–
  Jew / by Adam Woog
    p. cm. — (What Makes Me A?)
Includes bibliographical references and index.
Summary: Discusses Judaism including how Judaism began, what Jews believe,
and Jewish ceremonies, holidays, and food.
  ISBN 0-7377-2266-5
  1. Judaism—Juvenile literature. [1. Judaism.] I. Title. II. Series.
  BM45.W66 2004
  296—dc22
                           2003020951

Printed in the United States of America

CONTENTS

CHAPTER ONE

How Did My Religion Begin?

J udaism, the religion of the Jews, is one of the oldest religions in the world. In fact, it is the oldest of the three major religions that believe in a single God. The others, Christianity and Islam, have been strongly influenced by Judaism.

Father of the Jews

Judaism began almost four thousand years ago with a man named Abraham. Abraham was born in about 1800 B.C. in Mesopotamia, in what is now central Iraq.

Abraham's father was a maker of idols. Idols were statues of gods, such as mountain gods or river gods. Abraham's people worshipped many gods.

But Abraham questioned these beliefs. He wondered if there really were many gods. To go against his people in this way was unusual. Still, Abraham decided that only one God made the universe, and that only one God should be honored with prayer. Abraham gathered around him a small group of people who believed as he did.

One day, Abraham had a vision. In the vision, God told Abraham to take his people to a new land. God said that if Abraham obeyed this command, his descendants would become a mighty tribe. Abraham agreed. This promise was the first of many important

Abraham leads the Hebrews on the journey to their new homeland of Canaan.

The Cradle of Judaism

→ Abraham's Journey
→ Moses's Journey

Mediterranean Sea

CANAAN

Jerusalem

Dead Sea

MESOPOTAMIA

EGYPT

SINAI PENINSULA

Nile River

Mount Sinai

Red Sea

agreements between God and Abraham, or between God and Abraham's descendants.

A New Land

Abraham and his wife, Sarah, and the others in their group became known as the Hebrews. The Hebrews set out for their new land. After many years, they finally settled in Canaan, hundreds of miles from Mesopotamia. Canaan covered roughly the same area as Israel does today.

Abraham continued to lead his people for many more years. After his death, Abraham's son Isaac and his grandson Jacob led the Hebrews. Jacob had twelve sons, and each in turn led his own tribe or family. Together, these tribes were known as the Israelites. (This name honors Jacob, who was also called Israel. The name *Jew* honors Judah, one of Jacob's sons.)

The Israelites prospered for many years. But then a famine (a time when there is no food) forced them to leave their country and go to Egypt, a land to the west.

At first the Israelites were welcomed, but in about 1300 B.C. they were forced to become slaves. The reasons why are not completely clear. This slavery was the beginning of a long history of bad treatment, or persecution, of the Jews by other people.

The Egyptian rulers forced the slaves to worship their many gods. As the years passed, the Jews almost forgot their old religion and their belief in one God. But then a new Jewish leader, Moses, had a vision. In this vision, God told Moses to ask the pharaoh, the Egyptian king, for freedom.

"Let My People Go"

Moses said, "Let my people go," but the pharaoh refused. God then sent ten hardships, or plagues, as punishment. Among these plagues were swarms of pests such as lice and locusts. The worst plague killed Egypt's firstborn sons, including the pharaoh's son. However, the firstborn sons of the Jews were not killed.

This frightened the pharaoh, and he agreed to let the Jews leave Egypt. According to tradition, Moses led six hundred thousand men and their families away.

This journey, called the Exodus, took the Jews through the desert, back toward Canaan. It should have taken only about eleven days. However, the most direct route was blocked because the Jews could not travel through the lands of powerful rulers. Instead, they had to take a journey through the desert that lasted forty years.

During this time, God gave Moses stone tablets bearing holy instructions called the Ten Commandments. These laws were, and still are, Judaism's most important instructions on how to live a moral and correct life.

The Jews eventually reached Israel, where they created a strong nation. They prospered for hundreds of years under a series of kings including Saul, David, and Solomon. Solomon built a beautiful temple, or place of worship, in the city of Jerusalem. It became the holiest site of the Jews.

Moses receives the Ten Commandments from God. Following these commandments helps Jews and Christians lead moral lives.

King Solomon prays in his temple in Jerusalem. The temple was later destroyed by invading Babylonians.

Scattered

However, the Jewish nation fell on hard times after Solomon died. First, Israel split into two warring groups. Then, in the sixth century B.C., another nation, Babylonia, invaded. The Babylonians destroyed the Temple, conquered the Jews, and took many of them away to become slaves.

The united tribes of Israel thus became separated from one another for the first time. As time went on, the Jews were forced to scatter even more because enemies invaded their homeland and took control.

The Jews traveled to many distant parts of the world, looking for safe places to live. This wandering was called the Diaspora, a word that means "scattering."

Over the next centuries, the Jews were separated far apart, and they no longer had a homeland. But they never forgot their beliefs: their belief in one God, and in themselves as a people.

CHAPTER TWO

What Do I Believe?

Three books contain the basic laws and beliefs of Judaism. The most important of these books is the Torah, which Christians call the Old Testament.

The other books are the Mishnah and the Talmud. The Mishnah comments and expands on the Torah, and the Talmud does the same for the Mishnah.

The Torah, Mishnah, and Talmud tell many stories. These stories illustrate basic ideas in Judaism. For instance, one story tells how Moses worked as a shepherd for a flock of sheep. One day he brought them to a river so they could drink. One small lamb did not come, so Moses carefully carried it to the water.

The story shows that Moses was kind to animals. But it also shows that, like God, Moses cared about each individual in his flock, not just the group as a whole. This was why God chose Moses to lead his people.

The Basic Belief

All three of the main books of Judaism were written in Hebrew, the ancient language of the Jews. Using these texts as a basis, Judaism takes many forms. There are so many variations on Judaism that it is impossible to create one description that will define all Jews. This is because Jews disagree with each other on many points. In fact, there is an old saying that there are seventy ways to interpret every word in the Torah—and each way is correct!

A Jewish boy holds the scrolls of the Torah, also known as the Old Testament. The Torah contains Judaism's most important writings.

Still, all Jews can agree on a few basic points. For example, Judaism's most basic belief is that there is only one God. This is reflected in Judaism's primary prayer: "Hear, O Israel! The Lord is our God, the Lord is one."

More Beliefs

Many other beliefs grow from this one basic belief. For example, Jews believe that God alone created the universe and everything in it. They believe that only God should be worshipped. They believe that God is eternal and all-powerful. And they believe that God knows everyone's thoughts and deeds.

Jews can also generally agree on some other beliefs, such as the importance of the Ten Commandments. These are basic instructions that show Jews how to worship God and treat other people with compassion and respect.

Judaism teaches that everything in life and in the world is an example of God's greatness. A person's life should therefore be dedicated to praising God, and also to improving the world whenever possible. There is a strong emphasis in Jewish culture on making the world better by doing good deeds and improving oneself through study and worship.

Jews believe that everything that happens, even ordinary events, should be an occasion to thank God. An example of this is the use of the mezuzah. Mezuzahs are small, decorated boxes that contain holy passages from the Torah. These boxes hang near the front door of a Jewish household. (Some families put them in every doorway of the house.) One tradition suggests that people touch the mezuzah whenever they enter or leave the house. That way, even an everyday event such as coming in or going out reminds them of God.

Orthodox

Because Judaism takes many forms, it is often compared to a tree. Its basic beliefs are like a tree trunk, with many different branches growing out. Each branch represents a different way to be Jewish, and so each branch represents a different way to act and live.

Orthodox men dress in dark clothes and wear hats, while women wear long dresses and cover their heads with scarves or hats.

The three main branches of Judaism are called Orthodox, Conservative, and Reform. Orthodox Judaism is the strictest of the three. In Israel, nearly one-fourth of the population is Orthodox, but in America and elsewhere only a small number of Jews are Orthodox.

Orthodox Jews carefully obey more than six hundred laws given in the Torah, Mishnah, and Talmud. These rules determine such things as ways to pray, dress, observe holidays, and prepare and eat food.

For example, Orthodox men dress in dark clothes, grow beards, and always wear hats as a sign of respect to God. Orthodox women cover their heads and wear long dresses because they believe that they should not show their bodies or hair to anyone except their husbands.

Also, Orthodox Jews normally pray at least three times every day. And they often set themselves apart from the world at large by living in tightly knit communities.

Conservative and Reform

According to Orthodox Judaism, the Torah is the direct word of God and its laws can never be questioned. However, other branches of Judaism feel differently. For instance, Conservative Jews believe that the laws governing Jewish life can change over time.

Conservative Jews are thus less strict in observing traditional rules. For example, they do not wear special clothes or live in special communities set apart. Also,

In contrast with Conservative or Orthodox Jews, Reform Jews, like these children studying the Torah, are less strict about observing traditional laws.

unlike Orthodox Jews, Conservative Jews generally pray only on the Sabbath (the day of rest) and on holidays.

Reform Jews are even less strict. For example, Reform Judaism has removed or changed many parts of the traditional Jewish prayer services, to make them fit better with the modern world.

Conservative and Reform Jews are also less strict than Orthodox Jews in their opinions about how Judaism is passed down in a family. Orthodox Jews believe that any person whose mother is Jewish is also a Jew. However, according to Conservative and Reform Judaism, any person whose mother or father is

Jewish is also a Jew, as long as that person has been raised in the Jewish tradition.

The Messiah

Judaism shares many beliefs with another major religion, Christianity. However, there are also many differences. The key difference concerns the Messiah.

Both Judaism and Christianity teach that a great leader, called the Messiah, will bring the world together in peace and harmony. Christians believe that Jesus Christ was the Messiah. However, Jews believe that Jesus was a great teacher, but not the Messiah. They are still waiting for the Messiah.

CHAPTER THREE

How Do I Practice My Faith?

J ews have many ceremonies throughout the year to celebrate their faith. Some ceremonies are observed at home. Others take place in a house of worship. The Jewish house of worship is called a synagogue or temple. Some ceremonies are for the whole community, while others mark special moments in an individual person's life.

At Home

Families are important in Jewish life, so many ceremonies take place at home. Sharing in these rituals helps families remain close.

One example is the Sabbath, the weekly day of rest from work. Not all Jews observe all Sabbath traditions. However, those who do follow many special customs.

The Sabbath begins every Friday evening at sunset. Families mark it with prayers and the lighting of two candles. These candles symbolize joy and holiness. They also represent two holy commandments from the Torah. These commandments tell Jews they must remember the Sabbath and follow the traditions that keep it holy.

The Sabbath is not only a time for rest, but also for spiritual learning and reflection. Because it is a special

A girl and her mother light the Sabbath candles. The Sabbath is a period of rest and prayer that begins every Friday evening and ends at sundown on Saturday.

time, people eat special foods. For example, they often substitute challah, egg bread shaped in a braid, for their regular bread.

The Sabbath is a time for quiet reflection, and strictly religious Jews do not work at all during it. This means they cannot do such tasks as cooking, lighting a fire, writing, riding in cars, or turning on light switches. Even pastimes such as watching TV or playing musical instruments are forbidden.

Although they cannot work, Jews do many other things on the Sabbath. Families often invite guests into their houses. They also visit friends, take walks, and play board games.

Sabbath ends at sundown on Saturday. To mark the end, families light a special braided candle. Its three braids represent three important parts of Judaism: God, the Torah, and the nation of Israel. Sometimes they also pass around a box of spices, because its good smell symbolizes the sweetness of the Sabbath day.

At the Synagogue

The Sabbath is also observed at the synagogue, with services on Friday nights and Saturdays. Sabbath ceremonies include a reading from the Torah. Each week, a different part is read out loud, so that in a year's time the entire Torah is heard. A rabbi or a member of the synagogue does this reading, and it is a great honor to be invited to do it.

Before the reading, there is a ceremony to take the Torah out of the special cabinet where it is kept. This cabinet is called an ark. The Torah, which is handwritten on beautifully decorated scrolls, is carried around the room so that everyone can see it before it is taken to the podium for the reading.

There are many other customs in the synagogue. For instance, men and boys sometimes wear prayer shawls called tallith. Tallith have long fringes on the ends. Wearing tallith reminds the wearers to follow God's commandments. Men and boys also wear small caps called yarmulkes. They cover their heads as a sign of respect to God. Also to show respect to God, women and girls often cover their heads and shoulders with scarves in the synagogue.

Important Ceremonies

In addition to group ceremonies such as observing the Sabbath, Judaism also has rituals to mark important times in an individual's life. For example, at age thirteen (for boys) or twelve (for girls), young people go through ceremonies to symbolically bring them into adulthood. For boys, this is called a bar mitzvah. For girls, it is a bat mitzvah.

A bar or bat mitzvah takes place at the synagogue. The person being honored recites part of the Torah and makes a personal speech. There is also a party afterward—and lots of presents for the bar mitzvah boy or bat mitzvah girl.

Other ceremonies mark other important moments in a person's life. For instance, in a traditional Jewish wedding, the bride and groom stand under a special

Men and boys wear prayer shawls called tallith and skullcaps known as yarmulkes while praying in the synagogue.

canopy called a chuppah. Its roof symbolizes that the couple will start a new life together in the same house, but its open sides show that the house will be open to the community.

During a wedding ceremony, the bride and groom share a cup of wine, to symbolize the life they will share together. The groom also smashes a wine glass with his foot. This symbolizes hardships such as the

A girl reads from the Torah during her bat mitzvah, a ceremony celebrating her passage into adulthood.

destruction of the ancient temple. It reminds everyone that even a joyous union like marriage can have times of sadness.

However, weddings, like bar and bat mitzvahs, are mostly happy celebrations. There is lots of dancing, eating, and drinking. Everyone tells the honored people, "Mazel tov!" Congratulations! Good health!

The End of Life

Death also has its own rituals in Judaism. Jews accept death as part of God's will and the natural end of life. Although not all Jews observe all the rituals concerning death, the dead are always treated with great respect, just as they were in life.

According to custom, a body must be buried within three days of death. During that time, the body remains at home, in a simple, closed casket. According to tradition, someone (usually a family member) stays with the dead person, and candles are kept lit. These customs are marks of respect for the dead.

After the funeral, the dead person is still shown respect. There is a special period of mourning, and every year, on the anniversary of the death, a ceremony honors the dead person again.

CHAPTER FOUR

What Holidays Do I Celebrate?

Judaism has many holidays during the year. Some are colorful and joyous festivals that celebrate good things. Others are serious and quiet times.

The Jewish religious calendar begins in the fall. There are two main cycles of holidays—in the fall and again in the spring. These holidays fall on different days each year because the Jewish calendar is based on the movement of the moon, not the movement of the sun.

Rosh Hashanah

The cycle begins every fall with the new year, which is called Rosh Hashanah. It comes in September or October.

Rosh Hashanah is a day of rest. Traditionally, much of it is spent at home. One of the holiday's customs is to eat a meal that includes apple slices and bread dipped in honey. This symbolizes the hope that the next year will be sweet and that there will be many blessings for the family.

Part of the day is also spent in synagogue, listening to a special service used only on that day. At the synagogue, an important ritual is to listen to the shofar. This is a trumpet made from a ram's horn. An expert in playing this difficult instrument must make three different sounds and a total of one hundred blasts in a specific order.

A boy blows on a shofar. Listening to the shofar is one ritual of Rosh Hashanah.

Jewish Celebrations Throughout the Year

Purim
Celebrates the Jewish escape from the Persian Haman.

Passover
Commemorates the exodus of Jewish slaves from Egypt.

Shavuot
Celebrates receiving the law of God on Mount Sinai.

JANUARY   FEBRUARY   MARCH   APRIL   MAY   JUNE

Rosh Hashanah begins a period in the Jewish calendar called the High Holy Days. This is the most important period in the Jewish religious year. It ends with Yom Kippur, ten days later.

Yom Kippur

Yom Kippur is considered the most important holiday of the year. Its name means Day of Atonement. *Atonement* means apologizing, and being forgiven.

According to Jewish custom, the ten days before the start of Yom Kippur are a time for reflecting on how a person has behaved toward others. If someone has been treated poorly, this is the time to apologize and seek forgiveness.

28

Rosh Hashanah
Celebrates the start
of the new year.

Yom Kippur
A day to make
amends and ask
for forgiveness.

Sukkoth
Commemorates
the forty years of
wandering the
desert after
escaping from
Egypt.

Hanukkah
Celebrates the miracle
of a one-day supply of
oil burning in the
Temple of Jerusalem
for eight days.

| JULY | AUGUST | SEPTEMBER | OCTOBER | NOVEMBER | DECEMBER |

When Yom Kippur arrives, this day is set aside for thinking about behavior that might have offended God. People traditionally take part in a special service in synagogue. They pray for God's forgiveness and ask God to grant them a fresh start.

Also on Yom Kippur, people traditionally fast (that is, they do not eat or drink) for the entire day. One reason for this is to help people forget the body's needs so they can concentrate on spiritual needs.

However, there are exceptions to this rule. For example, children and people who are sick or pregnant cannot fast, even if they want to. This is because Jewish law teaches that preserving health is more important than observing even important rituals.

Hanukkah

One of the favorite holidays of young people is Hanukkah, which usually comes in late November or December. Although it is not one of the most important Jewish holidays, it is popular because it is a time of gift giving.

Hanukkah celebrates a miracle that happened after an ancient Jewish battle. The Jews regained control of the Temple in Jerusalem, and it was important to keep the holy flame there lit with oil. However, there was only one day's worth of oil. Somehow, this tiny amount lasted for eight days.

Children light the Hanukkah candles. Jews light candles each night during the eight nights of Hanukkah.

To celebrate this miracle, Jews light candles each night for eight nights. They light one candle the first night, two the second night, and so on.

To remind themselves of the miracle of the oil, people eat potato pancakes and other food made with oil. They sing songs and play games, such as a simple game played with a spinning top called a dreidel. Also, people exchange small gifts. Children often get chocolate shaped like gold coins—and sometimes real money too.

Passover

In the spring, Passover is the most important holiday. It celebrates a special event in Jewish history: the Exodus, or departure from slavery in Egypt. At Passover, people thank God for this great event. In this way, the holiday lets Jews worship God and remember their own history.

In addition to attending a service at the synagogue, at home people eat a special meal called a seder. Families and friends gather around a big table. The dramatic story of the Exodus is told while everyone eats many different foods that symbolize parts of the story.

For example, people eat a vegetable, such as parsley, that is dipped in saltwater. This represents the tears the Jews shed in slavery. Also, matzo is eaten instead of regular bread. Matzo is a cracker made only of flour and water. It reminds Jews that their ancestors left Egypt so quickly that there was no time to let their bread rise.

CHAPTER FIVE

What Foods Do I Eat?

Traditional Judaism has strict laws about what kinds of food can be eaten and how it must be prepared. These rules are called kosher laws. The most important kosher laws are in the Torah.

Each branch of Judaism treats these rules differently. Orthodox Jews are the strictest. Other Jews may or may not keep kosher, depending on their individual beliefs.

Why Keep Kosher?

To many people, Jews and non-Jews alike, kosher laws can seem confusing. The reasons behind them are not always clear.

Some scholars think that kosher laws were partly created out of health concerns. For example, in ancient times there was no refrigeration and food spoiled easily. Someone who ate spoiled food could get very sick.

Pork and shellfish were especially dangerous, and they are forbidden under kosher laws.

However, other laws do not have easy explanations. For example, without saying why, kosher law forbids eating a particular nerve in an animal's hindquarters. This means that many choice cuts of meat cannot be eaten, because the nerve is too difficult to remove.

Perhaps the best explanation for why some Jews keep kosher is simply that the Torah says so. Orthodox Jews consider the Torah the word of God, and that is reason enough to follow its laws, even if they cannot be explained.

Many Jews keep kosher, observing traditional dietary laws that restrict the types of food that can be eaten and how meals are prepared.

Meat and Fish

The Torah teaches that people should eat only certain kinds of animals. It allows meat only from animals that have cloven (split) hooves and that also chew their cud (that is, chew grass for a long time after they have first eaten it).

According to this rule, Jews can eat cow, lamb, deer, and goat meat. However, many other kinds of animals are forbidden. Among these are pigs, horses, and rabbits.

There are also rules about birds and fish. Some birds, including chickens, are acceptable. Those that are forbidden are mostly birds of prey, such as falcons and hawks. Meat-eating birds are considered unfit as human food because they eat other animals and because those animals might carry disease.

Any seafood that has fins and scales is acceptable. This means that most kinds of fish, such as tuna and salmon, are kosher. However, all shellfish, including oysters, clams, and shrimp, are not. Creatures that creep on the ground (or the ocean floor) are considered unclean.

Kosher laws also say how animals should be killed and prepared. A butcher must cut the animal's throat with a single motion from a very sharp knife. This ensures that the animal suffers as little as possible. Also, blood must be completely drained from meat before it can be eaten. The Torah teaches that the animal's life is in its blood, so eating meat that has not been drained of blood would be disrespectful.

Kosher butchers offer Jews a variety of kosher meats.

Keeping Milk and Meat Separate

Another important law is about the separation of milk and meat. Milk dishes are any foods made with dairy products such as milk or butter. Milk dishes must always be cooked and eaten separately from meat dishes.

This law comes from a passage in the Torah that says it is a sin to cook a baby goat in its mother's milk. The passage has been interpreted to mean that meat and milk should never mix.

Some foods are considered neutral. That is, they are neither milk nor meat. Among these are fish, eggs, and vegetables. Any neutral food can be eaten with a milk or meat dish.

Because milk and meat must be kept separate, maintaining a kosher household is somewhat compli-

A kosher kitchen has two sets of cookware and utensils in order to keep milk and meat dishes separate.

cated. A kosher cook must keep two of everything in the kitchen and dining room. There must be separate sets of utensils, pots and pans, dishes, glasses, and table linens. A kosher house does not need to have two kitchens if it has two sets of everything in this way.

Kosher cooks must shop carefully to make sure that everything is acceptable. Often, food in stores will be labeled to guarantee that it is kosher. Even boxes of crackers and bottles of juice may carry the symbol for kosher. That symbol is a "K" or "U" inside a circle. Also, many cities with large Jewish populations have special butchers, grocery stores, and restaurants where the food is always kosher.

Many Kinds of Food

Despite the strict laws, traditional Jewish cooking can be delicious. In addition to the special foods eaten at holidays, much of this is simply everyday food that has long been part of Jewish life.

Many traditional Jewish dishes originated in eastern Europe. Among these are chicken soup, borscht (a soup made with beets), and bagels (chewy, doughnut-shaped bread with a hard crust).

Other kinds of Jewish cooking comes from southern Europe, the Middle East, and North Africa. Typical of dishes from these areas are hummus, a dip made of ground, spiced chickpeas, and *hameen,* a spicy stew of meats, grains, and vegetables.

CHAPTER SIX

My Religion Today and Tomorrow

Judaism faces many challenges today. One concern is the possibility that the Jewish population may be shrinking and might one day disappear.

Falling Numbers

There are about 14 million Jews in the world today, mostly in America and Israel. That figure has remained fairly steady for some time, but Jews worry that their numbers are falling. They are concerned that Judaism's religious and cultural heritage could be lost.

Surveys show changes taking place among American Jews. Because so many of the world's Jews live in America, these changes could influence Judaism's future. Fewer and fewer American Jews now think of themselves as Jewish or attend synagogue. Also, more Jews are marrying non-Jews than ever before. Marriage outside the faith used to be unusual, but not anymore.

Nearly half of the American Jews who got married between 1996 and 2000 married non-Jews. Some of these mixed-marriage families will raise their children as Jews, but many will not. This means that the number of people raised as Jews will drop.

The future of Judaism does not depend only on American Jews. For Jews worldwide, the modern nation of Israel holds a special place in any vision of the future. Israel could be called the heart of the Jewish people and their religion.

Israel's Roots

Israel was founded in 1948. This event was connected to World War II and the Nazi Holocaust.

The Nazis were people who believed that "pure" Christian and Germanic people were superior to other

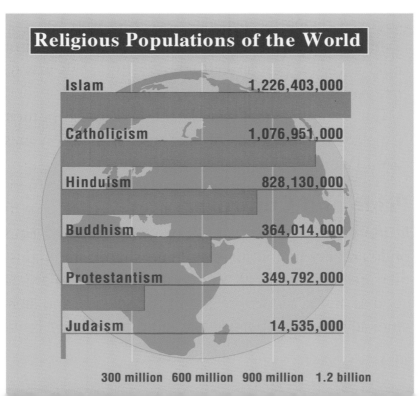

Religious Populations of the World

Religion	Population
Islam	1,226,403,000
Catholicism	1,076,951,000
Hinduism	828,130,000
Buddhism	364,014,000
Protestantism	349,792,000
Judaism	14,535,000

300 million   600 million   900 million   1.2 billion

races and ethnic groups. To them, the worst people of all were the Jews.

So, the Nazis took away the rights of Jews in Germany and other countries under their control. The Jews were sent to concentration camps, where they were murdered or allowed to die through starvation and disease.

In all, about 6 million Jews died before the Allies won the war. This tragedy was called the Holocaust, meaning a terrible slaughter of people.

Israel Is Born

The Holocaust had a powerful effect on Judaism. The movement to create a Jewish homeland, which had been active for years, received a big boost after the war.

For one thing, many Jews released from Nazi concentration camps had no place to go. Their homes had been destroyed during the fighting. Also, Jews who had survived the war wanted to make sure that the Holocaust could never happen again. One way to do this was to create a safe, protected country for the world's Jews.

That country, Israel, was established in the historic homeland of the Jews. At the time, this region was called Palestine.

Pride and Controversy

In the years since, Israel has been the source of great pride and inspiration for Jews. Israel's farms and industries are prosperous. Its schools and universities are as good as any in the world. Art, music, science, and literature all have an important place in Israeli society. Israel

Israel was established as a homeland for the world's Jews in 1948. Jerusalem (pictured) is the country's capital.

has once again become a strong nation, as it was long ago.

However, Israel is also the source of controversy and tragedy. For one thing, many different branches of Judaism are trying to control Israel's religious, political, and social life. They argue constantly with one another and create conflict.

Furthermore, when Israel was formed, many Arab residents of this region left or were forced to leave. These people, who call themselves Palestinians, also consider this land their sacred homeland. They have been fighting against the Jews to claim the territory.

As a result, violence between Israeli Jews and Palestinians has led to thousand of injuries and deaths. War has also erupted many times between Israel and neighboring Arab nations. Despite the efforts of many people to create peace in the region, a solution has not yet been found.

The violence in Israel deeply troubles Jews worldwide. There is disagreement over how to respond to the violence. Disagreement sometimes tears Jews apart. They fear the possibility of losing their homeland. They also fear a future without peace and stability in Israel.

Facing the Future

The issues of modern Judaism are serious. However, Judaism has survived many problems in the past.

Even in hard times, and even while they were scattered around the world, Jews remained hopeful that these problems would someday end. Meanwhile, their ancient traditions kept them united. As they face future challenges, Jews will continue to use these traditions to keep their religion and culture alive.

FOR FURTHER
EXPLORATION

Books

Michelle Edwards, *Blessed Are You: Traditional Everyday Hebrew Prayers*. New York: Lothrop, Lee & Shepard, 1993. This colorful book gives prayers for many occasions, including ways to pronounce them in Hebrew.

Doreen Fine, *What Do We Know About Judaism?* New York: Peter Bedrick Books, 1995. A nicely illustrated introduction to Judaism.

Bernard P. Weiss, *I Am Jewish*. New York: PowerKids Press, 1996. A very simple introduction.

Web Sites

Hilchos Shabbos (www.pirchei.com). This fun, illustrated guide to each step of observing the Jewish Sabbath is maintained by the Jewish children's educational society Pirchei Shoshanim.

Holidays on the Net (www.holidays.net). A site, maintained by a group in New York State, with information on holidays in many cultures and religions, including a lot on Judaism.

Jewish Funland (www.bus.ualberta.ca). This site has lots of games to learn the Hebrew alphabet and Jewish history and culture. It is maintained by Dr. Nurit Reshef, a teacher at a Jewish school in Canada.

INDEX

PICTURE CREDITS

ABOUT THE
AUTHOR

Adam Woog is the author of many books for adults, young adults, and children. He grew up in Seattle, Washington, and lives there now with his wife and daughter.